AF527692

ROLE OF HADITH

IN THE PROMOTION OF ISLAMIC CLIMATE AND ATTITUDES

Syed Abul Hasan Ali Nadwi

NADWI PRESS

NADWI PRESS

Nadwi Press Edition

Originally Published by AIRP, Lucknow (India)
Reprinted by Nadwi Press in 2025

Find our titles on your favourite online bookstore using the keyword 'Nadwi Press'

Translation of the Qur'ān

It should be perfectly clear that the Qur'ān is only authentic in its original language, Arabic. Since perfect translation of the Qur'ān is impossible, we have used the translation of the meaning of the Qur'ān throughout the book, as the result is only a crude meaning of the Arabic text.

Qur'ānic verses appear in speech marks proceeded by a reference to the Surah and verse number. Sayings (Hadith) of Prophet Muhammad (saw) appear in inverted commas along with reference to the Hadith Book and its Reporter.

Contents

In the Name of Allah, the Beneficent, the Merciful.

Preface

Praise be to Allah, the One, and Peace and Blessings upon the Prophet

This brochure contains a part of the extension lectures delivered under the auspices of the Rabita Alam Al-Islami, Mecca.

This Rabita organises, every year, a series of lectures by eminent scholars and thinkers of other countries coming to Mecca for the haj for the benefit of learned pilgrims as well as scholars of the city. These lectures are delivered in the spacious conference hall at the Rabita headquarters. The Secretary General of the Rabita, As-Shaikh Mohammad 'Ali Al-Harkan, desired me this year (1401 A. H.) to inaugurate the extension lectures and also to read an article on the imperative character of hadith. I accepted the offer gratefully but suggested that the topic needed to be slightly changed since a lot has already been written on the authoritativeness and authenticity of the ahadith. I referred to the valuable dissertation entitled *As Sunnatu wa Makanateha fit-Tashri al-Islami*, by my learned friend Dr. Mustafa As-Sabai, which deals with the matter in sufficient detail. I, therefore, chose the subject, "The Role of Hadith in the Promotion of Islamic Climate and Attitudes". As-Shaikh Mohammad Ali Al-Harkan and his colleagues in the Subjects Committee agreed to my suggestion and permitted me to write an article on the subject. It was thus that this article came to be read on Tuesday night, the 16th of Dhi Qada, 1401/13th September, 1981, before the scholars of Malik Abdul Aziz University, Mecca, and learned hajis hailing from different parts of the world.

I have tried to make out, instead, from a new angle, the significant place occupied by hadith in the life of the Muslims, its requisiteness for them, and the perils involved in ignoring or letting this invaluable patrimony slip from them. In this paper, I have tried to invite attention towards the present-day movements that have been set afoot by motivated persons in the world of Islam to discredit the authenticity of hadith and to create doubts about its authoritative character which constitute a deep-laid conspiracy against Islam. I have also referred to the ulterior motives of these traders of scepticism.

I have tried to avoid mentioning the oft-repeated arguments commonly cited in support of the hadith for much has already been written on the subject that would suffice to fill in a library. I have tried to keep before me the mental attitude and psychology of the modern educated class whose outlook and understanding have been moulded by the writings of Western orientalists and to which this class owes its knowledge in regard to hadith. This class keeps from delving deep into the intellectual discussions and shuns the definitive terminological concepts of the Islamic sciences. Nevertheless, it often asks: What is the practical utility of ahadith? Why should ahadith be deemed essential for the everyday life of the Muslims? What would be the harm, and what vacuum would be created in the life of individual Muslims and the community, at large, if ahadith were given up altogether? Often, these questions are expressly articulated and at times they remain troubling their minds. I have made an attempt to answer these questions, and I hope that deductive minds proceed not by theories and a priori arguments but by the logical relationship between the cause and the effect or, if I could say so, by way of mathematical equations, would feel satisfied after going through this article. It is, however, neither a research dissertation nor a magnum opus. Still, it does attempt to review the problem in a practical manner in the light of human psychology and factual evidence brought forth by our everyday experience and irrefragable testimony of history. I hope all those who go through this article without any preconceived notions and with a sincere desire to find out the replies to the aforementioned questions would feel satisfied. This article might help some of them realise the great importance of the hadith literature and arouse their curiosity to study it in depth.

Years back, I had thrown light on certain aspects

of the problem in an article written in Urdu.[1] It has now been incorporated into this brochure. The portion written in Arabic was translated into Urdu by Syed Salman Nadwi who accompanied me during my excursion to Hijaz. Thus prepared, this brochure was brought out by the Academy of Islamic Research and Publications a few months back. Now, its English rendering by S. Mohiuddin is being placed by the Academy in the hands of the readers. I humbly implore God that this booklet may be successful in achieving the purpose for which it has been written. Nothing would be more satisfying nor more meritorious in my view than being reckoned among those who have in any way served the cause of hadith.

S. Abul Hasan Ali
Daira Shah 'alam ullah Rae Bareli
12th Rabi- ul- Awwal, 1401.

---

[1] A part of this article was incorporated in my introduction to the second volume of Maulana Manzoor N'omani's Ma'arif- ul-Hadith.

Role Of Hadith In The Promotion Of Islamic Climate And Attitudes

Four-fold Objective of Prophethood:

The four-fold objective of the apostleship of Prophet Mohammad, specified by the Qur'an, comprises (i) recital of Divine Revelations, (ii) teaching of the Scripture, (iii) teaching of wisdom and (iv) purification of the people from all moral and spiritual filth. Says the Qur'an:

> He it is who hath raised among the unlettered ones an Apostle from among themselves, rehearsing unto them His revelations and purifying them and teaching them the Book and Wisdom, though they have been aforetime in error manifest.[1]

---

[1] Q. LXII:2

> Even as We have sent amidst you an Apostle from amongst you, who rehearseth unto you Our revelations and purifies you, and teacheth you the Book and wisdom, and teacheth you that which ye were not wont to know.[1]

The apostleship of the Prophet Mohammad covered these four aspects. The Prophet gave to the world a new Scripture and a new knowledge and wisdom in a like manner he bestowed upon it a new morality, a new and sublime thought and genius, a new faith, a new tenderness of feeling and devotion, a new generosity and noble- mindedness, a new spirit of self-sacrifice and solicitude for the after-life, a new concept of contentment and self-satisfaction, a new spirit of indifference towards the world and all that it stands for, a new ideal of love and benignity and compassion, a new delight in divine praise, a new ecstasy in the fear of the Lord and a new bliss in contrition and repentance of one's sins. These were

---

[1] Q. II:151

the bases on which the new Islamic society was raised, with an altogether new spiritual and moral environment, which is now commonly known as the era of the Prophet and his blessed companions. The companions of the Prophet were the finest representatives and shining examples of the ends and purposes for which God had sent the holy Prophet to the world. One desirous to see the aforementioned objectives of Prophethood manifested in the life of human beings should turn his eyes to this august body of godly men known as the Prophet's companions.

Formative Elements of Islamic Outlook:

The apostleship of the holy Prophet, his teachings and guidance constituted the fountainhead of all these blessings, and it was through his endeavour that the whole structure of life and society during the first century of Islam came into existence. But if the methodology and the ways and means employed for it were to be studied in depth and analysed it would be found that these three fundamental factors brought about this marvellous revolution:

1. The personality of the Prophet, his character and morals.
2. The Holy Qur'an.
3. The sermons, teachings and guidance of the Prophet.

These factors, a little thought would show these factors lie behind the entire manifestation of the ends and effects of the apostleship of the holy Prophet in the shape of a new community of believers. In fact, all three formative factors have played a decisive role in making the new ummah. This ideal society with a faultless social structure exhibiting a happy blending of faith and action, morals and emotions, likings and inclinations and human relationships would not have come into existence without these three formative elements. Life is a prerequisite of life; in our world, one lamp is lighted by another. The Islamic way of life informed by true faith and action, sublime morality, lofty idealism, and deep religious feeling, that we witness in the lives of the companions, was not due, simply, to the recital of the Scripture. A new life had been infused into them by the most perfect, effective and lovable personality of the Prophet. They always had their eyes fixed on him, profited from his noble company, and benefited from his guidance, teachings, and sermons. All these factors combined to fashion a distinctive Islamic outlook and temperament which responded not merely to legal commands and injunctions but was also moved by incentives to act upon those commandments; it had softer values of life and refined moral instincts which coalesced with the compliance of legal obligations, on the one hand, and deference to the limits set by God, on the other.

Effect of the Prophet's Company:

The companions of the holy Prophet had been commanded to *establish worship*[1]. They had also heard of the merits of those who are humble in their

---

[1] Q. II: 83

prayers[1]. Still, it was only when they performed their prayers in the company of the Prophet and witnessed his fervour and contrite heart in the state of *ruk'u* and *sajda* that they realised how supplication to God can take the shape of broken words of a heart struggling-up in trembling hope towards the Maker.[2] They had, no doubt, learnt from the Qur'an that prayer was the most favourite act with the believer. Still, they had no idea of the breathless impatience and avidness for it that was required of a believer until they had heard the Prophet saying, 'The coolness of my eyes lies in the namaz,[3]' and 'O Bilal! Give the call to prayer and bring comfort to my heart.[4] Likewise, they would not have appreciated the crush between the heart of a true believer and the Mosque until they had heard the Prophet saying that 'their hearts remained in the Mosque when they went out, and no peace had they

---

[1] Q. XXIII: 23

[2] Abu Dawud, Tirmidhi

[3] Nasa'i

[4] Abu Dawud.

until they returned to it.[1] They would have repeatedly read in the Qur'an the exhortation to cry to the Lord, or of the disgrace of those who did not implore Him for their needs. They would have also been aware of the significance of entreating, imploring and crying to God. Still, the underlying implication of these words would have only dawned on them when they saw the holy Prophet, in the thick of the battle of Badr, placing his forehead on the ground and entreating his Lord with the words, "O' Lord, I beseech thee, forget not Thy promise and covenant. O' Lord, if these handful of men were to be vanquished, idolatry will prevail, and Thou shalt not be worshipped."[2] They would have also noticed the anxiety and distress of Abu Bakr who was trying to comfort the Prophet and saying, 'It is enough, O' Apostle of God'. They knew that the life-breath of prayer was contrition and humbleness; the more one was broken in heart and spirit, the more precious

---

[1] Bukhari and Muslim.

[2] Sahih Bukhari, Kitab- al- Maghazi.

became one's supplication; but the true content of humbleness and meekness of heart would have been witnessed by them only when they would have heard the Prophet thus imploring the Lord on the mount of 'Arafat:

> "O' Allah! Thou heareth what I say, and seeth where I am, and knoweth whatever I conceal or reveal. Nothing concerning me is not within Thy knowledge. I am a sorrow-stricken destitute, crying for Thy succour and protection. I am crushed and scared, and I confess my sins. I acknowledge my wrongs and beseech Thee like a helpless supplicant; I implore Thee like a wrecked sinner like one humbled and abased; I lament before Thee for help like a sorrow-stricken, forlorn slave-like a man on bended knees, shedding tears, crouching in submission before Thee and licking the dust. O' Allah! do not leave me unheard and unanswered; be Thou compassionate

and kind to me; for, Thou art the Best among those who are merciful and the most Bountiful of all givers."[1]

Quranic Ethics:

The Companions had read in the Qur'an how transitory the life of the world is and how ever-abiding that of the Hereafter is. They also knew by heart the Quranic verse, *This life of the world is but a pastime and a game: Lo! the home of the Hereafter-that is life;*[2] but they could understand the real import of these words when they saw a living example of heart-felt conviction in this doctrine in the life of the Prophet. They saw the way of his life, his endurance and his frugal living as well as his extreme poverty and the hardships undergone by his household members and then, they understood what it meant to believe in the maxim: "O' God! There is no joy but the joy of after-life."[3] His was the shining example of a

---

[1] Kinz-ul-Ammal on the authority of Ibn 'Abbas.

[2] Q. XXX: 64

[3] Sahih Bukhari, Kitab- al- Maghazi.

life patterned on absolute trust in the life-to-come. With this illustration and trench- ant exhortations when they heard the Prophet portraying details of the blessings of Paradise and horrors of Hell, a transcendental feeling of fear mingled with eagerness was evoked within their hearts which produced a picture of the ultimate destiny of man-of one who was saved as well as of one who was doomed.

The companions were, in a like manner, conversant with the cardinal virtues like compassion, courtesy and good behaviour. They were an Arabic-speaking people and used also to ponder over the Qur'an but the full range of the meaning of these words and their application in practical life as well as the goodliness required for adherence to these virtues in action, became clear to them only when they witnessed the tender-heartedness of the Prophet in his dealings with the weak, the women and the children, the orphans and the needy, and the old, and finally, his behaviour towards his companions, friends, servants and family members. They had heard the Prophet's exhortations and admonitions. Also, they read in the Qur'an the divine command about fulfilling one's obligations to others, particularly towards Muslims. Still, there were numerous aspects of it like comforting the sick, joining the funeral and making prayers for the welfare of one who had even sneezed which could have never been conceived by any one of them as pertaining to good behaviour, nor anyone could have thought of the significance of innumerable paltry acts of charity. The Qur'an emphasizes the need to show kindness to one's parents and relations. Still, hardly any teacher of ethics would have ever thought of the sublime integrities of such teachings of the holy Prophet, as 'an excellent grade of dutifulness and kindliness to one's father is that a person does some favour to the friends and relations of his late father."[1] How many masterminds would have attained the lofty standard of generosity set by the Prophet as related by the Traditionists: 'It very often happened that a goat was slaughtered in the

---

[1] Sahih Muslim.

Prophet's house; he would have it cut into pieces and sent to the ladies friendly with his deceased wife Khadija.'[1]

These are a few examples of moral behaviour and social conduct taken from the Traditions of the holy Prophet. They can very well show the depth and comprehensiveness of the guidance provided by the Traditions in various fields of human behaviour as well as the insight they provide into human psychology. The worth and merit of the vast treasure-house of knowledge that these Traditions contain for humanity, at large, can be fully judged from just a few stray examples cited here.

Atmosphere needed for Virtuous Behaviour:

The history of religion is a witness to the fact that the injunctions and commandments are not sufficient in themselves to make the people act on them with the fulness of spirit required for complying with those commands. They simply do not

---

[1] Bukhari, Muslim.

create the right conditions and ethical atmosphere conducive to the moral behaviour of the people. The brief command to establish prayer does not, for instance, produce the mental awareness and conditions necessary for the preservation of its form and essence nor can it ensure constant observance or realisation of spiritual, intellectual, moral and social results required of the prayer. That an act of worship requires rules and formalities to make it effective and meritorious, the Qur'an has prescribed cleanliness, ablution, devotion, calmness, humility and congregation as some of the essential prerequisites for the observance of prayers. The more meticulously these external formalities, rules and rituals are adhered to the more an atmosphere tending to promote spiritual, mental and moral effects of prayer would be generated. Those who have studied the life of the Prophet and his sayings are aware that the directions and exhortations of the Prophet coupled with his personal example in this regard have so strengthened, and exerted such an influence, that the prayer has become the most efficacious instrument of self-purification, moral and spiritual perfection, sincere devotion to God to the exclusion of everything else in addition to making it a potent instrument of disciplining the community and infusing a sense of solidarity in it. The merits attached to ablution, its performance and intention; the virtues of bending one's steps to the Mosque and the blessings conferred on every step taken in that direction and the litanies recited during the course of it; the excellence of entering the Mosque in a proper manner; performance of orison after that and waiting for the service to begin; the blessings of the call to prayer and *iqamah*; the excellence of leading the service and grace of following the directions of the imam; the reward of keeping the rows straight; the goodness of teaching and learning within the mosque; the virtues of glorifying the Lord and His recollection; the etiquette of getting out of the Mosque and many more similar acts make the prayer a superb and solemn means of inculcating an awareness of God and reforming the morals of a man. Now, suppose we add to these the eagerness of the holy Prophet for the prayers, his readiness for supererogatory orisons, his absorption in the recitation of the Qur'an and his melting into tears in the course of its intonation, as related in the ahadith. In that case, it should not be difficult to imagine the aura of spirituality, piety and earnest devotion emanating from the prayers. The same is the case with every other act of worship like fasting, payment of poor-due and performance of pilgrimage. It should also not be difficult to visualize how for these devotional exercises would be able to retain their effectiveness and capacity to stir the feelings of reverence and piety and eagerness for attaining divine consciousness, or, for that matter, reforming the morals, or else giving rise to a spiritual-moral society if the events of the Prophet's life, his sayings and doings preserved by the ahadith were to be detached from them.

What we call hadith and the sunnah are the repository of the life and character, sayings and practices of the Prophet. They constitute the complex which provides the climate in which faith thrives and bears fruit. Religion is not a compendium of legal edicts, wooden and dry, nor can any faith retain its warmth of feelings without presenting living examples of its teachings which infuse a lifeblood into it's adherents. The most potent and authentic emblem of such events and emotions and their illustrations can be provided by a religion through the life-story of its founder. Judaism, Christianity and several other religions of Asia lost their inner vitality for the simple reason that they could not preserve reliable records of the life and character of their founders. Divested of this life-giving source they were deprived of that intellectual and spiritual climate which was necessary not only for the sustenance of faith and growth of religious spirit in the followers of those religions, but which could have also saved them from the onslaught of materialism and agnosticism. Some of them realised this shortcoming and tried to fill in the void with the manuals containing life-accounts, sermons and table-talks of their saints and holy men but these hagiographies eventually stuffed them with innovations and deviations distorting the very teachings of those religions. The bankruptcy of all these religions in regard to the genuine record of the lives and teachings of their founders is now an acknowledged historical fact.

Efforts to fill in the void:

This was the reason which led to the compilation of Talmudic literature[1] which caught the fancy of the Jews so powerfully that even the Pentateuch was relegated by it to a secondary place. Of a fact, there are several Jewish scholars on record who give precedence to the Talmud and recognise it

---

[1] Talmud is the standard collection of texts and commentaries on Jewish religious law, developed from the Pentateuch. It consists of two parts, the Mishnah and Gemara, the former being a commentary on the matters dealt with in the Mosaic legislation, and the latter a commentary on the Mishnah itself. In orthodox Jewry, the authority of the Talmud is held second only to that of the Old Testament, but according to the Jewish Encyclopedia, the Talmud shows that polytheism had a great attraction for the Jewish people (J. B. Vol. XI, p. 596 and Vol. XII, p. 690).

as superior to the Old Testament. The Talmudic literature codified between the third and the fifth centuries, naturally, incorporated a number of those extraneous concepts and legends that had gained currency among the degenerate Jewish society of the time, and which were no better than superstitions and folklore. It reminds one of the Quranic revelation that they measure not Allah His rightful measure.[1] The performance of the Christians has also been no better than the Jews; the additions made to the synoptic gospels are numerous as, for example, the Acts of the Apostles, the Epistles of Paul to the Romans, Corinthians, Ephesians etc., Epistles of James, Peter and John and the Revelations of St. John.[2]

---

[1] Q. XXII: 74.

[2] Even at the beginning of the fifth century, the Syrian church did not accept the minor Epistles or the Apocalypse. These were not added to the Syriac Bible until the sixth century. At the same time, in some Nestorian circles ,they probably were never

Hindus, from the ancient times, have revered the Gita consisting of the sayings and sermons of Sri Krishna. Their two more religious books added later on were the Ramayana and Mahabharata; the former is the life-story of Sri Ram Chandra, while the latter is an epic of ancient India. The same is true of the Zoroastrian Avesta and its priestly commentaries known as the *Vendidah* and *Bundahish.*

None of these scriptures succeeded in giving any exact information about the life and character of the founders and earliest propagators of these religions, nor has any of these scriptures been of any help in creating an urge among the followers of these religions to maintain and safeguard the original thoughts, beliefs and traditions of its religious pre-cursors. In fact, they did more harm to their adherents than doing any good to them. These books contaminated their religious thinking, led them astray from the natural path of God-consciousness

---

adopted at all. (A New Standard Bible Dictionary, London, 1926, p. 614).

and strengthened superstitious beliefs among their followers. The language and literature, thoughts and concepts of the followers of these religions were influenced by these books much in the same way as their social institutions, inclinations and passions were moulded by them. One can further trace the path of this drift. These books have gradually turned these religions into an admixture of superstition, mythical lore, and specious reasoning in which their original teachings constitute a mere drop in the bucket.

Biographies of the Prophets:

A comparison between the extant biographical literature relating to the Prophet of Islam and other prophets of old reveals the will and purpose of God. Anyone undertaking such a comparative study is sure to notice that the chronicles of the earlier prophets and founders of religions have been lost in the abyss of time, either owing to the ignorance and carelessness of the ancients or were consumed by bloody revolutions.

This, in itself, clearly indicates that the prophets of yore did guide the people of their times and showed them the path of virtue and goodness, but their teachings were not meant to be preserved for all times to come.

What has been stated here can be verified by looking closely at the narratives about Jesus Christ's life He was the last apostle of God before Prophet Mohammad, and his followers have always been known for their intellectual curiosity and academic achievements. Their unbounded love for Jesus Christ is also beyond doubt, for they have put him on the pedestal of divinity. Still, the Christians have succeeded in presenting only a sketchy and truncated picture of their Prophet which does not reveal his features clearly. Nor these accounts are complete enough to offer any guidance to an individual or society to pattern its life after him. The world of Christendom held the view till recently that the books of New Testament contain an account of the last three years of Christ's ministry. Biblical experts have, however, now reached the conclusion that the total span of events pertaining to the life of Jesus Christ narrated in the Gospels add up to no more than fifty days.

A contributor to the Encyclopaedia Britannica, Rev. Dr. Charles Anderson Scot, writes in his article on Jesus Christ:

> "The attempt to write a 'Life of Jesus' should frankly be abandoned. The material for it certainly does not exist. It has been calculated that the total number of days of his life regarding which we have any record does not exceed 50."[1]

It can thus be safely concluded that all the records and annals throwing light on the life and teachings of

---

[1] Encyclopaedia Britannica, 14th Edition, Vol. XIII. pp. 16/17. An other scholar and philosopher, Albert Schweitzer who has surveyed the whole enterprise from the earliest to modern times about the life of Jesus Christ in his monumental work The Quest of Historical Jesus begins the first chapter with the words, "There is nothing more negative than the result of the critical study of the life of Jesus."

the prophets and founders of earlier religions lie buried under the debris of irrecoverable past and the links connecting their life-stories with their teachings have been so completely lost that it is now not possible to follow in their footsteps.[1] This verdict of history is really consistent with the Divine Will and Wisdom governing this cosmos for we see that almost every great man who has appeared on the stage of history has been a shining example for others, but only for a limited period of time. The morals and values associated with every one of them lost their utility with the passage of time and then it became needless for subsequent generations to continue wedded to them or to emulate their examples. But, so long as a thing remains of profit and service to humanity its abiding nature keeps it unaltered even in the ever-whirling wheels of change. It remains firm and sound, defying all the changes and chances of mortal life.

---

[1] It would be worthwhile to go through Chapters II, III and IV of Muhammad-The Ideal Prophet by Syed Sulaiman Nadwi.

The attestation of history to the truth of Islam is also set forth by the fact that it was never confronted with a situation posing a danger to the survival of its original teachings. The intellectual and spiritual milieu and the psychological air in which the companions of the Prophet passed their lives have been preserved forever through the hadith. Later generations can find themselves transported, even after a passage of several centuries, to the times when the holy Prophet lived and preached. One can see the Prophet talking to his companions, their undivided attention and regardful attitude in carrying out his commands, their faith and trust in the Prophet's ability to transform their lives and morals and their conviction in the life after death that gave a direction and purpose to their existence. It is a window through which one can see the household of the Prophet his family life, his avocations during the night and the way his family lived. The ahadith allow us to lay our eyes upon the Prophet prostrating before the Lord and hear him glorifying God with tears flowing down his cheeks;

see his swollen feet on account of the night-long vigils and prayers, and overhear him silencing the enquirer by saying, 'What! shall I not behave as a thankful servant should."[1] How can anybody remain heedless if he comes to know that very often no fire was lighted in the Prophet's house for months together; he used sometimes to tie slabs of stone on his stomach to mitigate the pangs of hunger; rough mattress left the marks of reeds on his bare back; his restlessness on one occasion for not giving away a piece of gold before retiring for sleep; and, that lamp oil had to be borrowed from a neighbour during his last illness. How can one forget the worthlessness and fleeting nature of the terrestrial world and not take the lesson of frugal living if one gets an occasion to see the simple living of the Prophet? Anybody who can see the Prophet helping his wives in household chores, fondling the children, rendering service to his servants, behaving courteously with his friends, and showing kindness even to his enemies will never

---

[1] Bukhari and Muslim

think of gleaning knowledge about virtuous living and morality from anyone else.

The opening afforded by the hadith is not confined to the Prophet alone; we can see through it his companions also; how they spent their lives within their houses, how they laboured during the day and recollected God after the nightfall. We can take a look at them while they are transacting their business in the market, or have gathered in the mosque, or while they are performing deeds of selflessness, or when they have been led to commit a mistake and are broken in spirit by the sense of their guilt. One can direct one's eyes to Abu Talha Ansari when he put off the candle and made out like eating until his guest had taken his own meal.[1] One can also see through this opening how K'ab bin Malik failed to join the expedition of Tabuk and how he acknowledged that his own indolence was the only reason for not making necessary preparations to join

---

[1] Bukhari and Muslim. According to Ibn Kathir verse LIX: 9 was revealed on that occasion.

the expedition. One can also witness how he was put to a severe test before being pardoned. One can listen to his agonizing story in his own words through the ahadith.[1] Likewise, we find the incident of Ifak told by the mother of the faithfuls, 'Aisha, in a unique manner which bespeaks of her sensitivity, injured pride, truthfulness and firm belief as well as the elegance and grace of her speech-it is in fact a piece of literature that can be compared with the finest composition of any language. We also find, side by side, the story of exemplary forbearance and magnanimity of her father Abu Bakr in regard to Mustahab. Athatha narrated in the ahadith. In it we can see the human weakness exhibited by Hatib. Balt'a on the occasion of conquest of Mecca. The story throws light not only on an individual's failing and his error of judgement but also demonstrates that nothing has at all been concealed in the ahadith. Alongwith it, the incident speaks volumes of the unbounded forbearance, appreciation of past

---

[1] Sahih Bukhari, *Kitab- ul- Maghazi.*

services and the patronage extended by the Prophet to his friends and companions. It is a story that should find a place in the manuals of ethics for it has a lesson for every leader and reformer.[1] In short, the ahadith have pre- served in vivid colours a portrait of the life and times of the Prophet with a speaking likeness of the variety and realness of human life.

The preservation of this living picture of the Prophetic era, along with the Qur'an, conserving the backdrop, incidents and utterances of the holy Prophet is a distinguishing feature of Islam; it is something of a divine grace not allowed to any other religion. A faith which was meant to be eternal, which had to provide practical guidance for the emotional, intellectual, moral and spiritual behaviours of coming generations to the end of time could not have preserved its vigour without conserving its original settings, air and environs. The history of hadith demonstrates that the way it has come to be preserved for the posterity did not work out

---

[1] For details see Sahih Bukhari, *Kitab- ul- Maghazi.*

fortuitously nor was it because of any unwitting 'novelty' of the subsequent generations. The companions of the Prophet took meticulous care to memorise and even record the ahadith, the next generation tenaciously clung to retain this treasure, and then their successors turned to codify and arrange the entire record. Thereafter a legion of scholars came from Iran, Khurasan and Turkistan which memorised, collected and collated the entire literature with unbounded zeal; produced scholars who gave birth to the science of biography and critical analysis of hadith; created an urge for its learning in every heart; and was also rewarded for it by an appreciation of its efforts and popularity in the whole world of Islam.[1] All these developments make it self-evident that Providence had already decided to preserve ahadith like the Qur'an.

---

[1] For detailed study see Maulana S. Manazir Ahsan Gilani's *Tadwin-i-Hadith,* published by Majlis Ilmi, Karachi.

Perspicuity of the Ahadith:

I would do better to cite here a passage from the monumental work *Muhammad-The Ideal Prophet* by Syed Sulaiman Nadwi.

"There is, also, a sympathetic Christian biographer John Devenport, who begins his biography of the Prophet entitled *An Apology for Mohammad and Qur'an* with an acknowledgement of the fact that of all the law-makers and conquerors there is not one the events of whose life are more true and more detailed than those of the Prophet Mohammad."

"R. Bosworth Smith, late fellow of Trinity College of Oxford, delivered a series of lectures on Mohammad and Mohammadanism under the auspices of the Royal Institution of Great Britain in February and March, 1874. He says in his lectures, which were later enlarged and published under the same title: 'And what is true of religions, generally, is also true, unfortunately of those three religions which I have called, for want of a better name, historical and their founders. We know all too little of the first and earliest labourers; too much, perhaps, of those who have entered into their labours. We know less of Zoroaster and Confucious than we do of Solon and Socrates; less of Moses and Buddha than we do of Ambrose and Augustine. We know indeed of some fragments of Christ's life: who can lift the veil of thirty years that prepared the way for the three? What we do know indeed has renovated a third of the world and may yet renovate much more; an ideal of life at once remote and near; possible and impossible, but how much we do not know! What do we know of his mother, of his home life, of his early friends, of his relation to them, of the gradual dawning, or, it may be, the sudden revelation, of his divine mission? How many questions about Him occur to each of us which must always remain questions?

"But in Mohammadanism everything is different; here instead of shadowy and the mysterious we have history. We know as much of Mohammad as we do even of Luther and Milton. The mythical, the legendary, the supernatural is almost wanting in the original Arab authorities, or at all events can easily be distinguished from what is historical. Nobody here is in doubt of himself or of others; there is the full light of day upon that that light can ever reach at all."[1]

The authenticity and historicity of hadith literature does not only fulfil the criteria of genuineness, perspicuity, itemization of events, and preciseness but also baffles human intellect. No effort of a similar nature has ever been made by man to preserve the record of events pertaining to the greatest of men including the Prophets, nor the records of history furnish any parallel to it. Let alone the biographical records pertaining to the life of the Prophet, even a cursory glance on the books written on ahadith and personal character of the Prophet would be sufficient to clinch the point. One may examine, for instance, the ahadith relating to the last pilgrimage of the holy Prophet. It would be seen that they descend to such particulars as can hardly be

[1] S. Sulaiman Nadwi, Muhammad, The Ideal Prophet, (Lucknow, 1976), pp. 66-67

known even from the most detailed account of any con- temporary personality. These ahadith enter into such de- tails as how the Prophet applied perfume after putting on ihram; who helped him in it; what type of perfume it was; how he scratched the sacrificial animal as a token of its being sacrificed; where and how he did it; whether the animal was scratched on the left or on the right side; how the blood was wiped; whether the Prophet had taken recourse to phlebotomy; in which limb be allowed the blood- letting; where and how phlebotomy was performed; at how many places he made camp during the journey between Madina and Mecca, where he camped and in how many days the journey was completed; these and similar other minute details would be forthcoming from these ahadith although these were compiled during a time when people were not used to keep any diary or engagement book. One can even find in them the incident when a snake suddenly appeared amidst a gathering and slipped unhurt without being killed by anybody. They also tell us the names of those fortunate persons with whom the Prophet shared his dromedary[1], the name of the barber who trimmed the Prophet's hair, how he distributed his trimmed hair, who got the hair of the left side and who of the right, and, in a like manner, whatever he said, commanded or exhorted can be seen exactly in his own words in the ahadith. All this was done dutifully in compliance with his command: 'Whoever of you is present should convey it to those who are absent; perhaps those who may learn it indirectly may remember it better than those present.'

The sayings and practices of the holy Prophet constitute a standard, an exact scale by which the later reformers and revivalists of faith can measure the doctrines and disciplines and the norms and usages of public life of their own times and can find out the errors and deviations made by the community during its long journey through time and space. Likewise, it is essential for the right and proper

---

[1] In the Nasim-ur-Riyaz, the names of 38 persons honoured by holy Prophet in this manner have been mentioned.

functioning of public morality and virtuous behaviour of the individuals that both the Qur'an and the ahadith should be kept in view to draw out the rules of conduct. Had there been no record of the Prophet's instructions and his public and private conduct, exerting a steadying and moderating influence, the followers of Islam would have, like the adherents of other religions, gone to the extremes in their beliefs and observances and strayed from the middle and narrow path. Thus, a living personality, rather than an abstract maxim is held up as an ideal to set the pace in Islam. The Qur'an tells the Muslims: *Assuredly in the Apostle of Allah* you have an excellent pattern,[1] and urges them to take his life as a model in every little detail with the soul stirring words: Say, If you love Allah, follow me: Allah will love you and forgive your sins.[2] The holy Prophet of Islam is, in truth and reality, the great exemplar needed by

---

[1] Q. XXXIII: 21

[2] Q. III: 31

mankind for gaining strength and confidence in walking the path of virtue and goodness.

Hadith: A Censor of Morals

The actions and sayings of the Prophet are life-giving, effective, and weighty, which have always helped the people to exercise self-criticism and urged them to fight against iniquity and evil, deviations and innovations in the religious norms and usages of the private and public. life. They have given birth to virtuous persons in every age and country who have taken upon themselves the task of reform and revivalism, relentlessly fought superstitious beliefs and erroneous doctrines, and invited the people back to the Islamic way of life. The ahadith of the Prophet have, for that reason, always remained the sheet-anchor of every Muslim community: their diligent preservation, propagation and study is a prerequisite for the continuity of social, cultural, intellectual, moral and spiritual standards of Islamic way of life.

The truth of the matter is that the sunnah of the Prophet, preserved in numerous collections of ahadith, has always been the fountain of genuine Islamic thought and the passionate desire to reform and renovate the Muslim society. It was the hadith from which the reformers born from time to time were able to get an accurate knowledge of Islamic faith and thought; from it they acquired their thesis and arguments and on it they have always relied upon for the defence of their stand. It has also been the inspirational force behind their fervid enthusiasm to invite the people back to the true faith and fight every unsound norm and usage. And so, it shall remain to the end of time for anyone desiring to take up a reformatory undertaking in order to forge a link between the lives of the people to-day and the perfect example of the holy Prophet. He shall have to take recourse to hadith if he wants to cater for the changing needs of society in accordance with the principles of faith and morality as enunciated by Islam.

Evidence furnished by History:

History of Muslim societies in different parts of the world bears witness to the fact that whenever the Muslims have neglected the study of hadith for a considerable length of time, new aberrations and innovations, extraneous doctrines and usages and foreign influences have found their way into the lives of the Muslims notwithstanding the existence of spiritual guides and religious teachers, on the one hand, and powerful and affluent Muslim kingdoms, on the other. These alien thoughts and practices have very often threatened to transform and distort the Muslim society on the pattern of an un-Islamic community of the pagan past, as if fulfilling the foreboding of the holy Prophet that 'you would follow in the footsteps of the bygone nations.[1] These have been the times when the lamp of reform and renovation seemed to be flickering.

Take for instance the religious and social conditions of Indian Muslims during the tenth

---

[1] Hakim, Mustadrak

century of Islamic era, when religious and intellectual circles in that sub-continent had almost severed their connections with the hadith and its authentic sources. They had, during the period, no contact with the centres of religious learning in Hijaz, Yemen, Egypt and Syria where the study of hadith was still pursued. Educational institutions in India were then vigorously cultivating *fiqah* (law), *usul* (jurisprudence), logic, and philosophy but unsound usages had gained popularity, heterodoxy was a common spectacle, and numerous unorthodox forms of communion with God had been invented.

In the third volume of the *Saviours of Islamic Spirit*, I have taken stock of the teachings of Indian mystics and written about the *Jawahar-i-Khamsa* of an eminent and popular Sufi Shaikh Muhammad Ghauth of Gwalior:

"The country was also unacquainted with the *Sihah Sittah*[1] and other authentic books of hadith. It was only in Gujarat that the contact with the scholars of Arabia had kept the people conscious of this branch of Islamic learning. Ali Muttaqi of Burhanpur and Muhammad Tahir of Patan had kept the torch of Traditions lighted in that part of the country and endeavoured to discredit innovations in the religious thought and usages. But the orientation of life in all its aspects as dictated by the authentic sayings and practices of the Prophet, attempted by these scholars in Gujarat, was unknown to other parts of the country, nor did the people know anything about the *Sihah Sittah*[1] or about the scholars who had devoted their lives to the study of hadith and rebuttal of unsound norms and usages. The Jawahar-i-Khamsa by a celebrated Shattari mystic, Shaikh Muhammad Ghauth of Gwalior, offers the best example of the then Sufi thought which was permeated with the indigenous theosophic doctrines and practices. The articulate structure of sufistic precepts and cults propounded in this book are based entirely on the supposed utterances of the earlier mystics or the personal experiences of the author who, it seems, did

---

[1] The six most authentic compilations of hadith.

not consider it necessary to deduce these precepts from any authentic collection of hadith or any book dealing with the Prophet's life and character. Being a collection of orisons for special occasions and for specific purposes, it includes supplications for offering *namaz-i-ahzab*. (prayer of the confederates), *salat-al-'ashiqin* (prayer of the lovers), namaz *tanvir-al-qabr* (prayer of the grave's illumination), and a number of other devotions and supplications meant for different months of the year that cannot be traced to any saying or doing of the Prophet of Islam.''[1]

The *Jawahar-i-Khamsa* is not a solitary example of this kind. In numerous biographical accounts of saints, hagiographies and collections of their table-talks one can find similar unauthorised practices commended by them. Of the times we are talking about such practices as complimentary prostration before the mystic Shaikhs and their graves, lighting of candles at sepulchral monuments, laying of wreaths on the graves of saints and showing the same

---

[1] S. Abul Hasan 'Ali, Saviours of Islamic Spirit, Vol. II.

reverential regard to them as to the holy mosque at Mecca, celebrations like musical concerts, keeping of fasts and offering sacrifices to propitiate the saints, holding of fairs to commemorate their birth and death anniversaries were a common sight-in most of these ceremonies the saints were so exalted as if they were co-sharers of God in governance of the world.

There were conditions when God brought forth Shaikh Ahmad b. Abdul Ahad Sirhindi Mujaddid Alf Thani (d. 1034/1625) and his descendants and disciples who offered a determined resistance against the un-Islamic practices, refuted the concept of *bidat hasanah* or virtuous innovations, criticized *Wahdat-al-Wajud* (Unity of Being), invited the people to pattern their lives in accordance with the sunnah of the Prophet, and urged them to discard every *bidat* (innovation) in religion. In one of his letters, the Mujaddid has made a memorable asseveration which needs to be written in letters of gold.

"My Lord! this friar is not accustomed to endure such observations which stir his Faruqi blood and do not allow him to think out any explanation by stretching their sense. Such things might have been acceptable to Shaikh Kabir Yamani or Shaikh Akbar Shami, but what we require is the testimony of Muhammad (peace and blessings be upon him) and not that of Muhyiuddin Ibn Arabi or Sadruddin Qunawi or Shaikh Abdur Razzaq Kashi. We require nass[1] and not the fus[2]-the conquest of Madina has made us independent of the Conquest[3] of Mecca[4]."

Sheikh Abdul Haq b. Saifuddin Bukhari of Delhi (d. 1052/1642), a contemporary of the Mujaddid, spent his whole life in the teaching and propagation of hadith in India.[5] Thereafter Shah Wali Ullah (d. 1176/1762), also of Delhi, and his worthy sons took up

---

[1] Lit. a demonstration; that is, a legal maxim derived from the Qur'an or hadith.

[2] Alludes to *Fusus -al- Hakam* by Muhiyuddin Ibn 'Arabi.

[3] The allusion is to Futuhat-i-Mukkiyah by Muhiyuddin Ibn 'Arabi.

[4] Letter to Imam Rabbani, Vol. II, letter No. 100.

[5] See 'Hakim S. Abdul Hai, *Nuzhat- ul- Khawatir*, Vol.V; Khaliq Ahmed Nizami, Hayat 'Abdul Haq Dehlavi.

the cause of teaching and preaching hadith and the Qur'an, of explaining the true tenets of Islam, and inviting the people back to the path of shariah. They left no stone unturned to popularise the *Sihah Sittah*, the six most authentic collections of *ahadith*, and give these books a prominent place in their curriculum which, ultimately, helped to make this country, far away from the cultural centres of Islam, such a seat of learning that it started attracting students of hadith from the lands far and near including even the Arab countries.[1]

The most extensive and powerful revivalist movement known to history in the entire world of Islam during the thirteenth century sprang up in India. Anyone desirous of knowing about it need go through only the literature on the reformist movement of Saiyid Ahmad Shaheed, which gave a new life to the Muslims of this sub-continent and produced such examples of virtuous conduct which

---

[1] S. Hakim 'Abdul Hai, *Nuzhat- ul- Khawatir*, Vols. VI & VII.

awaken the memory of the Prophet's companions.[1] The movement inviting the people to betake themselves to the sound practices of the faith revived numerous sunnah of the Prophet and uprooted very many superstitions, pagan practices, and innovations in religion owned and accepted by the then Muslims of India. After the Saiyid's demise thousands of persons carried forward his reformatory work with a missionary zeal.[2] It can be asserted with confidence that all this happened because of the sunnah of the holy Prophet and his Traditions. Had these numerous compilations of hadith, giving an insight into the difference between the sound and unsound creeds and usages, not been available to the scholars, the successive chain of reformers and revivalists from Shaikh-ul-Islam Ibn Taimiyah (d. 728/1328) to Shaikh-ul-Islam Muhammad b. Abdul Wahhab (d. 1206/1792) would never have come forth. Some of these virtuous souls who have lightened the annals of

---

[1] See S. Mohiuddin, Saiyid Ahmad Shaheed, His life and Mission; S. Abdul Hasan 'Ali, A Misunderstood Reformer.

[2] For details see *Nuzahat- ul- Khawatir*, Vols. VII & VIII.

Islam, were Allama Muhammad b. 'Ali Al-Shaukani (d. 1255/1839), Amir Muhammad b. Ismail of Sana (d. 1182/1768), Ahmad b. Abdullah Idris Husaini (d. 1293/1876), Maulana Abdullah Ghaznavi of Amritsar, Shaikh Muhammad Azam of Kabul (d. 1298/1881), Maulana Syed Khwaja Ahmad of Nasirabad (d. 1289/1872), Maulana Ghulam Rasul of the Punjab (d. 1291/1874), Maulana Rashid Ahmed Gangohi (d. 1323/1905), Maulana Husain' Ali of Mianwali (d. 1363/1944), and Maulana Ashraf Ali Thanwi (d. 1362/1943).[1]

A concrete example of the positively right approach produced by the study of hadith is furnished by Shah Muhammad Ishaq (d. 1272/1856), a grandson of Shah 'Abdul Aziz Dehlavi, who wrote the *Masail- i- Arbain fi bayan- i- Sunnata Saiyid- ul-*

[1] The life and achievements of a number of these may be seen in Vols. VII & VIII of the *Nuzhat- ul- Khawatir.*

Mursalin[1] in 1255/1839, in reply to certain questions posed by Muhammad Zaman Khan of Bhikampur, 'Aligarh. This tract in Persian courageously assailed those customs and usages which had gained universal approval of the Indian Muslims. The small booklet had immensely benefited the Muslims of India since thousands of Muslims were guided by it in giving up the unsound and polytheistic customs and practices relating to births, deaths and marriages in compliance with the Islamic injunctions. Prior to this booklet, Maulana Muhammad Ismail Shaheed had written a pamphlet under the title of *Izah- al- Haq As-Sarih fi Ihkam al- Mayyat wal Zarih* which is one of the best writings that discriminate between the practices falling in the categories of sunnah and unvirtuous innovations, but the treatment of the subject in this tract being scholarly, it was made use of by the learned alone. *Masail-i-Arbain*, on the other hand, being in a simple style and dealing with the customs

---

[1] Consisting of fifty pages and published first by the Mujtabai Press of Delhi, the brochure expatiated Islamic view point in regard to forty usages in vogue among the Indian Muslims.

and practices adopted by the people, was of greater utility to the commonality.

Similar examples of reformatory endeavours undertaken in other countries like Iraq, Syria, Egypt, Tunisia, Algeria, Morocco, Afghanistan, and Turkistan can also be cited.

If one were to go through the biographies and writings of the tenth and eleventh century scholars of Afghanistan, one would find that little attention was paid by the then scholars to the commendation of the sunnah, and repudiation of heterodox precepts and practices, nor was any effort made by them to analyse and investigate these issues. Then, Mulla Ali Qari b. Sultan Muhammad Harvi (d. 1014/1605) suddenly appeared on the scene, who went to Hijaz for the study of hadith under the reputed scholars. He returned after drinking deep in that branch of learning, and then he took up the task of expounding matters relating to hadith and fiqah, putting up a front against the unsound practices that were commonly in vogue and endeavoured to reform the society of its ills. His probity and courage led him to defend Shaikh-ul-Islam Ibn Taimiyah and to boldly affirm that the latter was a savant with a pious soul who should be reckoned among the saints of Islam.[1]

In Iraq Allama Shahabuddin As- Saiyid Mohammad Alusi (d. 1270/1854), the renowned author of the Tafsir Ruh-al-Ma'ani, and his grandson Mahmud Shakri b. 'Abdullah b. Shahabuddin Alusi (d. 1343/1925) distinguished themselves from other scholars of that country because of their erudition in hadith. Allama Jamaluddin al- Qasmi (d. 1332/1914) who wrote several scholarly works on hadith and tafsir[2] was out of line with other scholars of jurisprudence, philosophy, literature and history in that country because of the reformatory note discernible in his *Islah al- Masajid min- al- Bid'a wal Awaid.* The world famous Azhar University was in Egypt where there was no dearth of learned scholars

---

[1] Mirqat Sharah Mishkat, Vol. IV, p.27

[2] As, for example, the Tafsir Qasmi, *Qawaid at- Tahdith* which contains the *Mustleh al- Hadith*, etc.

but because of their in-difference to hadith,[1] a number of unreceived religious practices had taken root in that country: birth anniversaries of the Prophet and Saiyidna Husain, congregations to mourn the deaths of the saints, and many other unapproved practices current in the circles of mystics had gained popularity among the masses during the tenth century. The effectiveness and potentiality of hadith was demonstrated when Shaikh Mahmud Khattab Subki (d 1352/1933), a lecturer at Azhar University, raised the banner of reform and renovation. He founded an organisation for the purpose in 1330/1912, trained preachers and sermoners, traversed every city and town and did not take rest until the heterodox practices were given up and sunnah of the Prophet was given its due place in

---

[1] Syed Rashid Ridha had written in the introduction to Miftah Kanuz as-Sunnata that the study of hadith had been neglected in Egypt and Syria since the tenth century and by the fourteenth century this indifference had reached its limits.

the ritual worships held in the mosques.[1] In India, too, Maulana Abdul Hai of Firingi Mahal (d. 1304/1887), whose curriculum for oriental institutions still holds the ground in India and Afghanistan, is out of line with other scholars of his day because of his refutation of the popular but unaccepted customs and usages. This was owing to his deep study of the hadith which is reflected in his juristic opinions. In one of his writings, he has himself expressed his thanks to God for making him inclined to the study of hadith and fiqh."[2]

Continuity of Religious Outlook:

It was because of the hadith and sunnah of the holy Prophet that the Muslims have continued to possess an Islamic outlook and religious inclination. They have continuously been inheriting the same spiritual and intellectual patrimony of faith, which had been directly passed on to the companions by the

---

[1] The writer of these lines has been a witness to the success of 'Allama Subki's efforts. For details see his Sharq, Ausat ki Diary.

[2] *An- Nafi- ul- Kabir*, p.154

Prophet of Islam. This uninterrupted continuity has been maintained not only in the creed and forms of worship and legal injunctions but has also had a constant flow in the shape of mental attitudes, moods, and tempers. Its perpetuation was, of a fact, made possible from one generation to another owing to the preservation of hadith, for there has never been any interlude, not even of the shortest duration, when this continuity was totally broken. In every age, there had always been some godly men who had been the inheritors of the companions' way of thinking and looking at things, their sentiments and dispositions. Such virtuous souls had exhibited the same zest for devotions, the same awe of God, the same steadfastness and trueheartedness, the same courtesy and humanity, the same self-control and equanimity, the same eagerness for the Hereafter, the same indifference to the world and all that it stands for, the same spirit to enjoin the good and forbid the wrong, the same aversion to every innovation in religion and the same ardour to follow every sunnah as had been instinctive with the companions of the

Prophet. All these virtues were either drawn from the study of hadith or by keeping company with those who had drank deep at the prophetic fountainhead. This frame of mind has persisted since the earliest period of the Islamic era down to the fourteenth century, notwithstanding the fact that the modern times have been overgorged with materialistic profanity.

So long as the hadith literature exists, it will continue to be read and studied, and thereby the air and feeling of the time of Prophet's companions will stay on. This will preserve the true spirit of religion, which gives precedence to the Hereafter over the worldly existence, to the sunnah over the unreceived rites and customs, and to the spiritual perfection over material benefits. This will save the followers of Islam from surrendering completely to worldliness and materialism, from setting their seal on the denial of life after death and yielding to innovations and deviations in religious matters. The hadith would always be giving rise to reformatory movements, and there will ever remain one or the other group upholding the true faith-putting its life on stake for maintaining the authority of sunnah and the shariah. It is because of this reason that those who want to rob the Muslims of this great reservoir of guidance and puissance try to create doubts in the authenticity of the ahadith. Perhaps such persons do not know what harm they are inflicting upon the ummah and how they are depriving it of such a precious and great treasure. They are not aware how they are unwittingly trying to disinherit the Muslims from their patrimony, which will eventually result in taking them away from their pristine creed and tenets in the manner Christians and Jews were led away from their faith by their enemies, or else they lost them through the vicissitudes of fortune. If these persons are wilfully addressing themselves to this nefarious task, then they are the greatest enemies of Islam and Muslims. For there is no other means to revive the feel and touch of the climate obtaining during the times of the Prophet's companions. This climate flowed directly from association with the holy Prophet, and now it can again be generated by the hadith, which is a living portrait of the Prophet's life.

Motive behind the Rejection of Hadith:

Muhammad Asad, (Formerly Leopold Weiss), an European convert to Islam (who is aware of the mental attitudes of the modern generation and also fully conversant with the imperialistic objectives and cultural domination of the West), has thrown light on the motive behind rejection of hadith, which is raising its head again nowadays. He has reached the conclusion that the norms and values of modern Western degenerate civilization, its way of life, and prevailing taste can never be in line with true spirit of Islam as reflected by the sunnah of the holy Prophet. Nor a life based on deep attachment to the Prophet and complete trust in him and his teachings as well as confidence on the reliability of hadith and its sources can ever be compatible with the concept of Western civilization's invincibility and the infallibility of modern categories of rationalism. This is perhaps the reason for rejection of hadith by certain politicians and administrative heads of Muslim countries who have already yielded the palm to modernism. Writes Muhammad Asad:

> "In these days, when the influence of Western civilization makes itself more and more felt in Muslim countries, one motive more is added to the strange attitude of the so called "Muslim intelligentsia" in this matter. It is impossible to live according to the sunnah of our Prophet and to follow the Western mode of life at one and the same time. But the present generation of Muslims is ready to adore everything that is Western, to worship the foreign civilization because it is foreign, powerful and materially brilliant. The "Westernisation" is the strongest reason why the traditions of our Prophet and, along with them, the whole structure of the sunnah have become so unpopular today. The sunnah is so obviously

> opposed to the fundamental ideas underlying Western civilization that those who are fascinated by the latter see no way out of the tangle but to describe the sunnah as an irrelevant, and therefore not compulsory, aspect of Islam-because it is "based on unreliable traditions". After that, it becomes easier to twist the teachings of the Qur'an in such a way that they appear to suit the spirit of Western Civilization."[1]

Thus, all those persons who are hand in glove with the rejectors of hadith or are trying to shake off its authority, worth and value, are really insensible to the great disservice they are doing to the Muslims. Muhammad Asad has correctly identified the real motives of this conspiracy against Islam since he says:

---

[1] Muhammad Asad, Islam at the Crossroads, (Lahore, 1963). pp. 129-30

"The sunnah was the iron framework of the House of Islam; and if you remove the framework from a building can you be surprised if it breaks down like a house of cards."[1]

Asad has also drawn attention to the inevitable consequence of denying the authority of ahadith and decrying the need of following the Prophet in all walks of life. He says:

"And in this way, the exceptional position of Islam as a moral and practical, as an individual and social code, would be shattered to pieces."[2]

The people trying to create distrust in the authority and authenticity of hadith as well as those inviting the people to reject it altogether have had different motives and personal, religious or political ends to serve during different periods of history. Some of them have, on the other hand, foolishly abetted such activities simply to get away from

---

[1] Islam at the Crossroads, op. cit. p. 113.

[2] Islam at the Crossroads, op. cit., p. 129.

certain obligations of the shariah or moral and religious restraints.[1] Yet, notwithstanding these efforts, the sunnah of the holy Prophet has always remained imperative and weighty and a shining example inviting the people to betake the path shown by it. That an Islamic society is made up of a texture consisting of hadith which permeates through every pore of the body-politic of Islam, it would be well-nigh impossible to separate it from any Muslim community. Nor it is possible to form a new Muslim society, complete in all respects, based solely on the Qur'an. The purpose of holy Prophet's apostleship has been made clear by God in these words: *And we have revealed unto thee the remembrance that thou mayest explain to mankind that which hath been revealed for them.*[2]

---

[1] For a detailed description of such activities see the second chapter of *As-Sunnatu wa Makanateha fi-Tashri al-Islami*-by the autho

[2] Q. XVI: 44.

Study of hadith literature along with its critical investigation and annotation and research and publication of old manuscripts has continued at all times without a break. Similarly, its abiding imperiousness has been the determinative force in a critical evaluation of the norms and usages of public life, in the summons to betake the path of virtue, in the bidding of the good and prohibition of the evil, in confutation of innovations and deviations in religious creeds and practices, in restraining the people from blind imitation of Western civilization and in acting as a check against intellectual, cultural and religious apostasy of the masses. Next to the Qur'an it has all along been regarded as the most authoritative source of the principles of faith. The hadith has, in this manner, fulfilled the prophecy made by the Apostle of God that a section of his followers would always stick to truth down to the Day of Judgement.[1]

---

[1] On the authority of Thauban and Muawiyah.

Thus, there is not the least doubt that all those persons who are trying to create a doubt in the authenticity and authority of hadith in order to secure rejection of the Prophet's sunnah are frittering away their energies in a fruitless task. *Fain, would they put out the light of Allah with their mouths, but Allah will perfect His light however much the disbelievers are averse."*[1]

---

[1] Q. LXI: 8.

www.ingramcontent.com/pod-product-compliance
Ingram Content Group UK Ltd.
Pitfield, Milton Keynes, MK11 3LW, UK
UKHW021359190726
13845UKWH00028B/773

9 789394 770645